BOOKS BY NORMAN DUBIE

The Horsehair Sofa   (1968)

Alehouse Sonnets   (1971)

Prayers of the North American Martyrs   (1974)

Popham of the New Song   (1974)

In the Dead of the Night   (1975)

The Illustrations   (1977)

A Thousand Little Things   (1978)

The City of the Olesha Fruit   (1979)

Odalisque in White   (1979)

The Everlastings   (1980)

The Window in the Field   (1982)

Selected and New Poems   (1983)

The Springhouse   (1986)

The Springhouse

W · W · NORTON & COMPANY · NEW YORK · LONDON

The Springhouse

POEMS BY Norman Dubie

Acknowledgment is due the following publications, in which these poems first appeared:

The American Poetry Review: "Hummingbirds," "Leda & the Swan," "Nine Black Poppies for Chac," "The Widow of the Beast of Ingolstadt," "Meister Eckhart," "The Diamond Persona," "The Funeral," "Letter to Rue Robert de Flers," "Danse Macabre," "Through a Glass Darkly," "An Annual of the Dark Physics," "The Woolen Lamb," "Lamentations," "The Williamstown Gulf," "Sanctuary."
Antaeus: "The Elegy for Integral Domains," "The Duchess' Red Shoes."
The Antioch Review: "Dream."
Argos, Wales: Old Night and Sleep.
Crazyhorse: "La Pampa," "The Trolley from Xochimilco."
Field: "New England, Springtime," "Wintry Night, Its Reticule."
Hayden's Ferry Review: "The Train."
The Mississippi Review: "The Huts at Esquimaux," "Oration: Half Moon in Vermont."
The New Yorker: "New England, Autumn." © 1984 by *The New Yorker Magazine.*
The Pacific Review: "The Lion Grotto."
Telescope: "Archangelsk," "Provence."

Epigraph from *Homage to Mistress Bradstreet* by John Berryman © 1956 by John Berryman © renewed 1984 by Mrs. Kate Berryman. Reprinted with permission of Farrar, Straus & Giroux Inc.

This work was supported by a grant from The National Endowment for the Arts.

Published simultaneously in Canada by Penguin Books Canada Ltd, 2801 John Street, Markham, Ontario L3R 1B4
Printed in the United States of America.

The text of this book is composed in Bulmer, with display type set in Bauer Bodoni. Composition and Manufacturing by Maple-Vail Book Manufacturing Group. Book design by Antonina Krass.

First Edition

Library of Congress Cataloging-in-Publication Data
Dubie, Norman, 1945–
   The springhouse.
   I. Title.
PS3554.U255S7 1986   811'.54   85–29714

ISBN 0-393-02302-8
ISBN 0-393-30323-3 (pbk.)

W. W. Norton & Company, Inc., 500 Fifth Avenue, New York, N.Y. 10110
W. W. Norton & Company Ltd., 37 Great Russell Street, London WC1B 3NU
1 2 3 4 5 6 7 8 9 0

For Jeannine

Contents

1. The Diamond Persona

2. Sanctuary

3. Lamentations

PART 1

The Diamond Persona

We are on each other's hands
Who care.

—John Berryman

Hummingbirds

They will be without arms like God.

By the millions their dried skins will be sought
In the new world.
Their young will be like wet slugs.
They will obsess the moon
Over a field of night-flowering phlox.
Their nests will be a delicate cup of moss.

In pairs
They will feast on a tarantula in thin air.

They have made a new statement
About our world— a clerk in Memphis
Has confessed to laying out feeders
Filled with sulphuric acid. She says

God asked for these deaths . . .   like God
They are insignificant, and have visited us

Who are wretched.

3

The Elegy for Integral Domains

You watched the slender narcissus wilt
In the vase below the pulpit.
You could never explain how the brain
Was packed with light, or that memory of a circus:
White undigested bone in tiger filth. The fear
Suddenly let go of you while you watched
The rich jeweler in the pew
Across the aisle. His hair fell down
That side of his face where the eyepiece stayed—
You wondered about skin wrinkled
From looking at jewels,
And then the fear left you with the wind
Over the pond, with the swelling
Of the church organ. There was the sweet smell
Of boiled corn in a cold night kitchen. The risible
Life of a spider living in a dry cracked flute,
And fog, you wrote, in the straw of the universe.

We can never be the undoubted stone.
Dice and mathematics. Music and the storm.
You loved the reticence of something
Heard first from the oboe. Some secret
Not heard from the solo instrument. And
Then runs of it in the orchestra. You heard of Schumann
In the asylum at Endenich near Bonn,
The white Schumann sprawled on the bed,
The attendant flicking at the tube to the enema bag.

You loved your wife, but the undoubted stone
Has no life in it. The diamondback pattern
On the cloth of the hose to the vacuum cleaner
Ran in and out of time, ran
From your mouth to the exhaust of the Plymouth.

Your brother gave me your journal, asking me
To write this. It made a hag of me in a night.
You loved life.
There is no way someone can make himself ready

To say this: a man dragging
A Christmas tree out of the woods found a body.

5

Leda & the Swan

It was her time in the month—
A matter of luck, Leda had a corruption.
It was the only problem, but he was a god.
It put him off. So the wife of Sparta
Swam to the seclusion
Of the riverbank and collapsed, unconscious . . .

It wasn't Leda he took but a slave girl
Who was bathing with her in the water.

With the beak he held her at the nape
And dunked her which is the instinct
With swans—
If she had struggled for very long
She would have drowned.
She loosened her body, he stiffened
And her eyes opened all of a sudden on river bottom.

There was a sound of wings rising backwards
Striking fronds. Leda woke
From what she understood to be a dream,
Three months later she died of plague.
The slave girl took air into her mouth;
Into her eyes she took a cruel god
Receding into sky like something thrown.
She had swallowed water. She had scraped her leg.

Helen of Troy and Castor were born in one egg.
Clytemnestra and Pollux in the other. The girls

Grew to know their true mother.

New England, Springtime

Emerson thought the bride had one eye
Boring into the dark cellar. You stand
In the dry tub shaking powder over your shoulders.
The neighborhood is busy.

It is like anxiety: housepainters dressed in white,
Two hold a ladder while the third climbs,
Drenched in sunlight they are blind travelers
In a vertical landscape of cut ivory.

On my mother's verandah the addled missionary drinks tea.
She says
That in India if a child is bitten
By a cobra, the villagers leave at the site
A saucer of milk and hibiscus flowers. She says
That in India there is fur on a struck bell
Like fur on a bee. A toad eats a fly.
A toad sleeps. Out in the cistern

There is the great gone stomach of algae.

While the missionary speaks, we drag
An open sheet of newspaper behind us, we rise
And then kneel, with a spade we are burying
The heads of sunfish in the roots of rosebushes.
It will feed the flowers. Emerson thought
His bride
Had her one eye on the cool hams in the cellar.

Later, on a walk, we stand on a train trestle
And hold each other:
We are lost watching the hot track reach back

Under the flowering trees, the track
Has white pollen on it to the vanishing point.
It is unsustainable in the long day,

Cattle cars rattling by at sunset.

Nine Black Poppies for Chac

I.

The junta was jubilant around the mortised fountain.
A solemn procession of century plants going to the bridge.
A dead chauffeur in the ditch.
                            You thought
You watched a quetzal bird fly from the bursting tin
Of gasoline. Nine enemies of the junta
Are sprawling in the back of an open Mercedes.
You threw your last two paintings into the sea. Looked
For snow on the mountain.
You washed your legs and breasts in a jagged fragment
Of mirrorglass. And wrote, *except for the groin,*
My body is seamless. I've changed my mind about God again.

II.

Near the shack your Winchester kicks once—
In your line of vision the lifting hawk did not drop
For it had eclipsed briefly a crow, your lead passed
Through its black stomach:
                            the hawk banks to the left,
Free falls, tucked
For one complete revolution, then wielding suddenly
Onto the immaculate screw of a rising thermal,
It rose a degree or two on the horizon and made
Its quick diagonal hit at the neck of the dead crow.
It took only a moment. You fed the chickens corn, and
Threw the Winchester into the ocean.
The dead colonel in the Mercedes wore his winter coat
Like a cape, arms absent from the sleeves. For this
You dislike him even more. The newspaper talked
About the contents of his mistress' stomach. The colonel
Had made a sautéed abalone.

9

Abalone, like inkfish,
Needs prodigious pounding with a pine mallet.
The red foot of this shellfish is butchered
Like a steak. When the fat reaches the point of fragrance
Cook two minutes to each side.

O, yes, parsley
To clean the palate first.
You hoped you had watched a quetzal bird flit
In and out, alongside the limousine,
Below the green stand of cane . . .

and a cavity
Was cut deep into the colonel's loins,
it was
Irrigating pink in the eternal spring rains.

The Widow of the Beast of Ingolstadt

A fork in the garden, the widow digging
Behind her elms
Lives like a mouse with the esteem of a few flowers.

She watches at dusk
While the indigo bunting, out of its cage,
Walks through a plague of snails
That is still smoldering. The gardener
Killed them with gasoline and a long trench, it was
Lye the last time. She thought

Of Pastor Bonhoeffer, who plotted
Against Hitler, and the other prisoners
In the canvas truck
That burned wood, the *chuff-chuff*
Of steam up the late winter road
From Buchenwald to Flossenbürg— all of
Them hanged in the morning, in the background
The white outbursts of an acetylene torch
Up in the eaves of the S.S. barracks . . .

The widow last night was reading
The third testament, just a row of birches
Swaying in the breeze, and she felt aged—

Then, in all of a moment, she knew
Her husband's watch had just stopped in his grave.

La Pampa

The dead truck sits in the shimmering wheat.
The vegetables on the sill were meant to go
To seed. Looking past them there is a tomb.
Beyond the tomb, in the heat, two boys
Enter a grove, they were told not to: in the branches
Is the drying skin of a black bull
Slaughtered that noon, the boys' father
Sits on the ground in the dripping shadow of the skin.
He is eating plums. Last night, their newborn sister

Slept beside the paraffin stove, their mother
Had left some of her milk in a cup
In the icebox, it was blue, sticky
And too sweet, they thought. Their grandfather
In fever spoke of the judges of the dead,
Of words of necessity:

                    a young librarian
Went straight in the chair, a tooth lost
In her upper lip. They were so silent
While they knelt there in the grove— they felt
It was just their luck that at the moment
Their father stood to dust himself off
The younger brother was seized, it seemed, by hiccups.
The next winter he fell into the well. Past midnight
The older brother remembers while the sergeant
Tortures the young librarian
In white pajamas and turquoise slippers.

Meister Eckhart

All day the snow festered
In the balsams

And then the sun set . . .
His great providence

Increased with furs, he shook
And vomited. He gnawed

Again at a cold wing
Of pheasant.

Outside the window, some
Poor farmers

Struggled in the yard:
A hog that died earlier

In the thaw of afternoon
Would not be subtracted

From the frozen mud
Through which it had ploughed

And lodged. The air
Was ecstatic with cold.

The bull of John XXII, dated
January 7, 1327, speaks

Of him as being, this night,
Dead. It says

He first renounced his heresies,
And then was lifted . . .

Eckhart, a mystic,
Had thought

That a stone to the extent
That it is being

Is greater than God, for
Being could not be subtracted

From it. That was his.
He taught that being aware

Of what God is not, we still
Are ignorant of what God is . . .

And creatures of themselves,
He said,

Are pure nothings.
Before the gathered Franciscans,

Before the Inquisition, he spoke
Of a love that seizes us—

While he spoke
The hemorrhage rose to his mouth—

Before the assembly
He concluded his defense, observing

That the last light
Was leaving their proceedings . . .

He choked back the blood, saying
That is enough for the present.

And he meant it.

Dream

It was the Sung Dynasty.
They wore pleated red jackets. Virtually children—
I saw that she had concealed
In her hand a quartz blade and something
Like the dark leaves of hepatica.
There had been torrential rains
For three days. The young couple had walked
All morning to reach a waterfall and its pool;
They now knelt before one another
In an ester mist rising from pitcher plants.

It was spring and the boy's father
Would tomorrow flee with his family inland
To escape invading Tartars.
The spider who lived behind the mirror brought
Good luck, his father had said; it died
The day the rains began. The rains had weakened
Cliffs of decayed limestone that were miles
Above where the couple had knelt
Beside a waterfall to kiss. I said she opened
Her hand, she held a tiny quartz knife
And mossy stonecrop. He nodded to her,
And the distant limestone cliffs with a hillside
Of firs slid down into the river, choking it.

The stonecrop fell to her lap. The river slowed,
And then
            the waterfall stopped.

The Diamond Persona

I dreamt Tolstoi was mad and running away
By train to the north.
My wife and brothers
Built for me a forty foot tower
With a platform of reeds where like St. Simeon
I either sat or stood
In all weather for more than six years.

The tower consisted of four rooted trees
Drawn in at their waists
By a diamond-shaped tourniquet of hemp,
The ropes went out in all directions at once
Like a desperate prayer
That brings emptiness and trembling and then
A centering peace.

Pails brought my meals and took away my waste.
It was rumored the Czar would visit.
By the first summer
The campfires stretched out for miles
At my feet. Ladders were hung from my tower
And peasants brought me children
To be healed; aristocrats and scholars
Asked in detail about my visions. By the second winter
I stopped all but the ritual meal of bread and cheese.
I bled like sleeves from a body. Over the years
The people forgot me.

Early in the last spring I knew
I was dying. I gave instructions to my acolytes
And by twilight my platform was soaked
In kerosene, the fire was set

And with one pass of a large French blade
A strongman from Mongolia cut
The fraying ends of the diamond tourniquet— burning
I flew into the heavens.

My body was found in a near field
And I was buried there.
My only regret is that our beloved mother
Abandoned us as children for literature,
Which gave us ideals, only soon afterward
To abandon literature for religion,
Only *then* deciding
That everything was meaningless

Except the life of her youngest son, who, in devotion
To his mother, would fly and burn like the sun
Above some fanciful future spring planting.

PART 2

Sanctuary

The Funeral

It felt like the zero in brook ice.
She was my youngest aunt, the summer before
We had stood naked
While she stiffened and giggled, letting the minnows
Nibble at her toes. I was almost four—
That evening she took me
To the springhouse where on the scoured planks
There were rows of butter in small bricks, a mold
Like ermine on the cheese,
And cut onions to rinse the air
Of the black, sickly-sweet meats of rotting pecans.

She said butter was colored with marigolds
Plucked down by the marsh
With its tall grass and miner's-candles.
We once carried the offal's pail beyond the barn
To where the fox could be caught in meditation.
Her bed linen smelled of camphor. We went

In late March for her burial. I heard the men talk.
I saw the minnows nibble at her toe.
And Uncle Peter, in a low voice, said
The cancer ate her like horse piss eats deep snow.

Archangelsk

The yellow goat in winter sunlight
Is eating a birch canoe.
The carrot fields are black.
Snow is falling like sawdust. Joseph Stalin

And his barber are in fine spirits
This morning. It is the first day of Lent.
They are laughing about a prisoner
Who in three nights of questioning
Confessed repeatedly
To having painted over
A fresh cocoon on a garden fence.

The prisoner
Is dying on a narrow canvas cot.
He has dragged his last shoe of coal
Through the camp. He did not die of the cold.
He died of typhus: crying first

For his sister, then for their yellow goat
Who ate asters
And finally for the lake cottage—
Bullets rippling like moles under the plaster.

Sanctuary

My sister got me the script. I couldn't
Believe it. To work for Charles Barzon.
He was doing a film of *Thérèse Raquin.*
Zola's novel. The wife is in love
With her sickly husband's best friend;
They are on an outing— an accident is staged
On the river. They drown
The husband. The river takes him.
Then begin
The visits to the Paris morgue:
Each day from a balcony
They look down at a flat, turning wheel;
Eight naked corpses, unclaimed,
Revolving on a copper and oak bed.
A fine mist
Freshening the bodies. I was
To be one of them. I almost said no.

But Barzon's a genius. He took us aside,
One at a time. He gave us
Secret lives, even though we were the dead.
I was Pauline,
A sculptor's model of the period.
I would have to shave my groin,
Armpits, and legs.
Hairless, Pauline was a strange euphemism.
What is the scripture,
The putting on of nakedness?

"You'll be like marble," Barzon said.

I felt a little sick
With the slow revolutions and lights.

The cold mist raised my nipples.
My hair was ratted and too tight.
Between takes, we shared from boredom
Our secret lives:
To my right was a ploughman, kicked
In the chest by a horse. He staggered,
Barzon had told him, out of the field
Into the millrace.
To my left, a thief who had been knifed
In a Paris street. We were spread-eagled,
Cold and hungry. I looked over to the thief
Who was, to my surprise, uncircumcised . . .
I said, "Verily, this day you will be
With me in Paradise." For a moment the dead
In their places writhed—
Barzon was so upset saliva flew from his lips.

The dream occurred that night. And every
Night since.
Three weeks now, the same dream:
One of the carpenters from the set
Is on a high beam way above us.
I don't know how I see him past the lights.
But there he is, his pants unzipped.
I scream. Barzon looks up from a camera
And says, "Get that son-of-a-bitch."
The workman slips
Just as a floodlight touches him.
Before he hits the floor, I'm awake.
The first thing I realize
Is that I'm not a corpse, not dead,
Then, in horror,
I see I am still naked and Thérèse Raquin's
Drowned husband
                is sitting accusingly at the foot of my bed.

The Duchess' Red Shoes

I.

after Proust

Swann has visited the Duc and Duchess de Guermantes,

And now he is walking his horse the first kilometer
Through the woods down to the road. It is his short-cut.
The two roads entering the Guermantes estates
First circle back before returning to the front gates
As if to ask

Whether or not to arrive correctly at Eight. One autumn day
Swann's drunken coachman, finding the north road
To the estates, fell asleep and the horses
Coming to the loop, not to be delayed,
Not wanting to saunter back through the gardens before
Making the gate, simply raised their heads, snorted
In the cold air, and with little difficulty

Ploughed through the Duchess' bed of champagne-marigolds,
White mud plastered their legs as they stopped before
An astonished black servant-in-livery.
And Swann with his laughter woke his coachman.
The coachman promising to shoot himself in the head
That very evening, only after saying good-bye
To his children.

Swann kissed the man's cheek and asked him to see that
The horses got sugar with their feed.

II. *The Visit*

The Duc and Duchess de Guermantes loved Swann. Their friend
Was always welcomed by them personally, even in the morning.

And now Swann is walking his sorrel horse back the first
Kilometer through dripping poplars—
Earlier in the day in a poor district of Paris
Swann had sat before a doctor who was eating
A potato with dried beef.
It was not even a matter of months! Days, perhaps, the doctor
Added, as he threw the potato peel out the window while
With the other hand reaching his napkin.

Swann said, "Oh, I see, then I'll be leaving you, doctor."
The doctor continued eating. Swann thought him refreshingly
Decent. The doctor looked up from his plate only after Swann
Had put a door between them. The doctor then reached
Into his shirt pocket for three fat radishes that
He had thought better of eating in front of this poor soul
Who was soon to be ashes in blue pottery that sits

in a gold plate.

III.

Swann had gone to the estate that afternoon to tell his
Friends he was dying. His friends were leaving
For a party.

"What's that you say?" cried the Duchess, stopping for
A moment on the way to the carriage. She was
Saying to herself, "He is dying?" The Duc, now,
Insisting they will be late for the party. Getting into
The carriage, her skirts raised, she heard her husband cry:

*Oriane, what have you been thinking of! You've kept on
Your black shoes. Where are your red shoes, Oriane?* He was

Rushing her back into the house. The Duchess saying, "But
Dear, now we will be late!" The Duc explains that proper
Shoes are more important than the hour of the day. Looking

Back, the Duc says to Swann, "I'm dying of hunger!"
Swann says that the black shoes didn't offend his taste.
The Duc replies, "Listen, all doctors are asses. You are
As strong as Pont Neuf. Now, Oriane, please hurry." Swann
Wonders if this was an expression of love, or courage?

Swann pauses in the woods to watch his friends' speeding
Carriage make that loop through the gardens—
The carriage tips this and that way. Suddenly from
The Duchess' window a pair of black slippers waves a
Farewell. Swann turns away.

IV. *The Duchess after the Burial*

Poor Swann, death, you know, is shy. Death says
That no one can take a bath for you.
And Swann, the Bishop would hate me for this,
But death says no one else can die for you.
Not on crossed sticks even with Romans tossing bones
Below you. Not in any circumstance. Oh, Swann,

Your horses went wild again— in the cemetery!
I thought the graves were opening. The Duc said as
We were leaving you, that day of the red shoes, "No one
Can eat, sleep, or make love for another."
I said, "Your mother when your were inside her ate for another.
A man with a worm eats for another. And often, dear,
A woman makes love for another who is her lover, customer,
Or husband."

Swann, your horses soiled the Bishop's gown
And destroyed the six fern-pots
Of Charlemagne's Cross, the Iron Stair of Violets

27

Looked more like a broken orchard ladder afterward,
And your hearse, missing its forewheel, stopped finally
In one of those shallow ornamental ponds.
There were dropped prayer books all over the ground.
Your horses, their work done, drank deeply from the pond.

Your wonderful, drunken coachman with a black bottle
Of beer raised above him
Delivered a strange and genuine eulogy, then falling
Backwards into the water in which your horses

Were peacefully urinating. I insisted we leave then.
The Duc said that you had not yet
Been placed in the ground. I said you had returned
To that element from which so much life has sprung—

The chaos of a small pond.

Provence

The knight walks along the deep brook
Nibbling at a rusted tiger-lily
Dragging his slipper through the grass
Where partridges are stilled, indistinguishable
From the dried cow manure.

The knight's young page
Is back in the orchard, asleep on the earth:
The reins of a giant horse are
Tied twice to his calf and ankle: the horse
Grazes dragging the dreaming boy
Through the yellowing fallen fruit of the orchard.

The knight and the boy both love
The lady in the tower above the gorge.
By dusk they will sit with her husband,
With a flacon of wine
And a standing rib in a platter of dark berries.
They will talk of the distant war

And of fealty to the lion.
Above them in the tower, the lady
With two girls attending
Washes her breasts and neck in lemon water.
She is holding a sponge from the Mediterranean.

At the table now the boy sleeps, the knight
Is unconscious with drink by the fire, and
The old man in the shadows, shaking daggers
From his wide sleeves, is their liege lord.
He is watching the airedales sniffing the young bitch
Who snarls and then whimpers off into the cooling kitchens.

29

Letter to Rue Robert De Flers

For David St. John

She dreams the sky is a monk's boiled milk.
The dusty road
Clears at the old circuit house
Just before the cholera
Checkpoint erected in her childhood.

It is your first day in Paris.

I was listening to the radio,
In the early evening outside Gare de l'Est
A bomb exploded
In a vegetable truck killing three
Tibetans and injuring their sister.
There is a dead sniper in Los Angeles.
Children are now fighting for the Persian Gulf
And our government is concerned that if the war stops
There will be an oil glut.

The dead Tibetans' sister is in a hospital
In a suburb of Paris.
She dreams she is under mosquito netting
Lacquered with her breath: at the foot
Of her cot are scattered rubbings
Made by her brothers at the stone feet
Of the sexual yogis of the temple
At Khajuraho: combs of hemlock, cobras

For ciphers and the twisting back
Of a woman— her breasts having frozen
The two flanking cobras, a hypnosis
Before milking— her legs are raised
In a straight line like the horizon.
The yogi is standing but crouched,
Her buttocks in the cup of his hands.

30

The cobras are surrounded by rhododendron trees—
When they blossom the catastrophe of milking begins.

An old nurse passes a lemon swab between her lips:
Metal, green vegetables, and the splintered wood
Of crates were shot through her body; she dreams
Of a cholera checkpoint, of rain at mid-day,

And easily now the sun heaves
Into the abandoned red ramshackle
Of the old opium warehouses
That slouch down the hillside into the Ganges.

Danse Macabre

The broken oarshaft was stuck in the hill
In the middle of chicory,
Puke-flowers, the farmers called them, sturdy
Little evangels that the white deer drift through . . .

Nobody on the hill before
Had heard of a horse
Breaking its leg in a rowboat. But the mare
Leapt the fence, passed
The tar-paper henhouse,
And then crumpled at the shore.

It was April and bees were floating
In the cold evening barn; from the loft
We heard them shoot the poor horse.
We tasted gunpowder and looked
While your cousin, the sick
Little bastard, giggled and got
So excited he started to dance
Like the slow sweeping passes
Of a drawing compass—

Its cruel nail to its true pencil.

New England, Autumn

Our daughter dreamt of magnolias—
That one mammal among flowers.

You dreamt of bluets
And the hearts of celery. The cat
Had dreamt of his old sock
And the black
Beetle scratching inside the matchbox.

We burned the toast.

The whole house peppered with the cold.
I missed the shadowy hardpan of the desert floor
With the smoke trees and palo verde.
You both asked about my dream.

It was evening.
My dead grandmother was in the yard
That sloped down to the pond;
She'd carefully placed a linen tablecloth
Over the clothes-horse for drying . . .

I watched a mosquito,
Which rose from the back of my hand
Heavy with blood, vanish
Into the caption of a saw-toothed mouth—
The old pike
Striking from under the lily-pads.

In a matter of seconds that blood had traveled
From my heart
To the very bottom of the chilled pond.

I woke with a start as if we had set an alarm.

Wintry Night, Its Reticule

There are suffering mice

Down low between the thatch, down
Where the wind lifts red berries
That float and roll with snow
Across a frozen marsh, young deer
Watch while a few berries
Drop into the green muck of their tracks—

The lady's-slipper with its fleshy sac,
The bones of a lost hunter strewn
Through sumac—

Spring, at last.

Through a Glass Darkly

after Ingmar Bergman

They are out bathing in the sea at night
With long white legs and arms, the fallen bones
Of the shoulders like heavy tack in the barn
That their ungoverned breasts swing from,
A silhouette of pine at the groin, ink
There and in the eyes,
The wet rope of hair down the back,
The buttocks coarse with the cold air
Like sack. They are my young cousins— insomniacs

Who have just come
From making love to their husbands.

With sand they first washed the seed
From their thighs. I sat on the rocks
And bit
Into the stiff salted skin of fish.

I want them to be this happy.

As children hiding behind the lilacs
We huffed together over the tiny iron file,
When we were done there was one brass tooth
Left on the spool of my mother's music box.
It wasn't much of a song but I taught it

To God while cowering behind the cold radiator
In the long hall of the hospital.
My dead mother was also troubled.
The novel of her death
Went to the publishers the day after she died.
My father's books are sold in six languages.

He hates this island.

My husband is a doctor, he has a nightmare
In which a neon light flashes
A caduceus and then a dollar sign.

He would leave Sweden. He still might.
My cousins have stepped out of the sea.

Looking exhausted
And heavy in their hooded robes,
The sand slowing them, they walk
Across to me like the Franciscans
Who escort us to and from shock therapy . . .

PART 3

Lamentations

The Williamstown Gulf

From a hill we watched the brown floodwater
Cross the immense snow plain,
A white sheet of paper slowly burning—
The flashboard of the dam burst
Taking the mortar-lip with it that morning.
The village was in no danger.
Under a limestone
Wall, in ice, we found
The red berries of Solomon's seal. We watched

Three frantic deer climb out of the ravine.
The game warden with his thermos of brandy
Was squatting down under the spruce trees.
The sun setting as we climbed into the car.

The wallpaper in our room at the Inn
Had whorled faces made by a leaky radiator
That shook the ceiling. Light from the window
Crossed your breasts, a nipple
Pink and erect through the loose cable-stitch
Of the black sweater. At the light switch
You stopped

And looked for the first time
Into the old photograph, an inscription
In white ink. It was the old garnet mine
At Morse Mountain:
                              a blind pit pony climbing
Out of the earth, the dirty splint on its leg
Wrapped night-eye to cannon bone, pan-candles
At his withers;
And then, a big grizzled man
In just long johns holding the blur

Of a frightened field mouse by the tail . . .

I asked, "What is it?" Beginning
To undress in the dark,
Your clothes falling over the chair, you stepped
Into what light there was in the room, light
That had come from the moon, and said,

"There's a giant in that photograph, cats at his feet,
One gold and one black, the gold cat
Is playing with a yellow stub of wax, the giant
Has taken just the tail of a mouse
Out of the mouth of the black cat— he dangled
It before him for the photograph. There's a pony
Who caught a pick-axe in the leg. It's the old talc mine
On Morse Mountain. I could never live like that . . .

I'd sooner eat the sleep of Solomon's seal."

The Trolley from Xochimilco

I.

The late afternoon rain stopped. The electric trolley
Did not. You looked up
From your pencil sketch of a bird's nest
Upset on the skull of a forgotten doge. The trolley

Struck the wooden bus at the center bench, the bus
Stretched forever and then burst—
The virgin of Guadalupe scattering with the pigeons.
A block away people had fallen in waves
Before the splintering wood. It was not raining
Anywhere in Mexico City. The Red Cross ambulance

Was coming. The collision
Took your dress:
A rail passed through your stomach,
They drew it out of you on the street, your scream
Opened rain clouds over the cathedral and shops.

A baker passed
With his intestines gathered in his arms. A painter's
Little packet of gold dust, mixed with your blood,
Made your body shocking to passers-by
Who felt they had seen enough.

You were eighteen and had proclaimed to friends
Over sherbet that you would
Have the baby of Diego Rivera. That night
Coarse with morphine you told the doctors

You lost your virginity at the corner
Of Cuahutemotzin and 5 de Mayo. They laughed,

You screamed like a horse . . .

II.

Death is the favorite doll of little girls. I saw
Her tonight standing on a heap of coal in Detroit.
I hate the gringo dream of being important. Their
Little cocktails honoring this and that *gran caca* . . .

But they buy Diego's paintings. I want a banquet
Of pulque and squash blossoms.
I have painted my long skirt, maroon and green,
And put it on a powder-blue hanger in Manhattan.

Kiss the little girl. I will always paint
For her with my eyes. A kiss
Is like a dress falling off a tall building.
I miss the monkey and the fence of organ cactus—

I will write more before we take the boat.
Sleep, your Frida will not cut Diego's throat.

III.

It is better to go, to go.
　　　—Frida Kahlo

It was an electric trolley from the floating gardens.
The first Indians to discover them
Were searching for food,
Were drugged by the scent of orchids, white mint,
And islands of gentian— when they woke
They found everything moved . . .

To the groin you were prepared with tinctures
For the operation: the ether became
Your favorite cartoon of a log being sawed.
Returned to the house,
In silence, you took a leg from each
Of the dolls, telling the large pail-baby, Diego,

42

Who still loved you, that it was a cruel revenue
Worthy of this government

That wore one white shoe. A great woman, and trouble!
They sent you flowers.
                    The flowers moved . . .

It was a reluctant telegraph of women, at dawn,
Passing from an upper bedroom, to the parlor,
To the foyer, to his man,
                    the old chauffeur
On the lawn with a handful of dead snails—
He crossed over to Diego, saying:
Miss Frida is no longer with us! A bird
Flew from the palms. It was a problem. For you
Had made him understand: our bodies

Are long. You touch me.
Our hands plunged in oranges:
You breathe, a tambourine,
My back arched, lifting off the sheets,
You are kissing my breasts, you are kissing

                    the plaster rosettes of the ceiling.

A Woolen Lamb

They cut the red threads—
They broke the voice,
　　but it is singing
Together with us,
Together under the suns,
It rises, your voice
　　of blood and song.
　　　　　　—*Victor Jara*

The blood complicates your hair, dark sienna and matted
Like the roofs of hillside huts . . . your strong nose,
And on the shirt over your corpse there's an insect:
A live, giant lacewing: one stilled lime-green wing,
And the other tipped wing is red, three of its legs lifted
Up out of the blood on your chest. Your chest, the
Open pits . . . dark mules with ore walking
A cliff road that winds down to the mines past the cool sheds.

In your hand there's a bullet, a bit of waxed string.
Along the coast of Mexico on the day of your death
A storm picked up a window box of tall roses
And drove them, individually, four inches into
An adobe wall in a village two miles inland, the
Great heads of these flowers were not hurt.
They live in this shaded wall that's carefully watered.
Like governments, death can decorate the dead: ice-green,
Lime-green and red. Victor,

Your songs are coal. And Chile sleeps the stubborn sleep
Of the horizontal rose
In its baked, day-white, vertical bed.

The Huts at Esquimaux

For Dave Smith

Our clothes are still wet from wading
The Chickamauga last evening.
There is heavy frost. We have
Walked on the dead all night.
Now in the firelight
We are exchanging shells and grape shot.

I can still hear our loud huzza
When late in the day
The enemy fell into full retreat
Along the pine ridge to the East . . .

We chased them until we were weary.
Each night this week
There's been something
To keep me from sleep. Just an hour ago
I saw

A dead sharp-shooter sitting
Against a rock with a scallop
Of biscuit still lodged in his mouth.
He wore one silk sock.

Snediker has returned from Chattanooga
With five thousand convalescents
For the left wing of their musketry.

We have roasted a deer
With a molasses sauce and pepper.
Magrill and Zandt have returned
From horse hunting with a sack of sugar.
By morning we will have buried our dead
And fed the prisoners: Joe Cotton

Will hang all seven of them in one tree
When he sees they're done
Licking their fingers . . .

I shot a Rebel yesterday
In high water just for cursing me.
Just six months ago
For that alone it would have meant
Three days in stockade.

We can see now that cannonading
Has set the hillside on fire.
The wounded Grays
Will be burned
Beyond their Christian names . . .

Joe Cotton says he'd ask God
For rain, but he's got no tent
And river water
Has chilled him straight through

To the very quick of his being.

Oration: Half Moon in Vermont

A horse is shivering flies off its ribs, grazing
Through the stench of a sodden leachfield.

On the broken stairs of a trailer
A laughing fat girl in a t-shirt is pumping
Milk from her swollen breasts, cats
Lapping at the trails. There's a sheen of rhubarb
On her dead fingernail. It's a humid morning.

Tonight, with the moon washing some stars away,
She'll go searching for an old bicycle in the shed,
She'll find his father's treasures:
Jars full of bent nails, a lacquered bass,
And the scythe with spiders
Nesting in the emptiness of the blade
And in the bow of its pine shaft.
Milling junk in the dark,

She'll forget the bicycle, her getaway,
And rescue
A color photograph of an old matinee idol.
Leaving the shed, she'll startle

An owl out on the marsh. By November
It will be nailed through the breast to the barn.

In a year the owl will go on a shelf in the shed
Where in thirty years there will be a music box
Containing a lock of hair, her rosaries,
Her birth certificate,

And an impossibly sheer, salmon-pink scarf. What
I want to know of my government is

Doesn't poverty just fucking break your heart?

An Annual of the Dark Physics

The Baltic Sea froze in 1307. Birds flew north
From the Mediterranean in early January.
There were meteor storms throughout Europe.

On the first day of Lent
Two children took their own lives:
Their bodies
Were sewn into goats' skins
And were dragged by the hangman's horse
The three miles down to the sea.
They were given a simple grave in the sand.

The following Sunday, Meister Eckhart
Shouted that a secret word
Had been spoken to him. He preached

That Mary Magdalene
Sought a dead man in the tomb
But, in her confusion, found
Only two angels laughing . . .

This was a consequence of her purity

And her all too human grief.
The Baltic Sea
Also froze in 1303—
        nothing happened that was worthy of poetry.

The Lion Grotto

Nothing odd.

The pink adobe wall holds the shadows
Of the children
Who have shucked oysters
Onto a fresh bed of shaved ice.
Behind them, out of nowhere,
Is the long straw-colored
Plumb line with its brass bob.

From the kitchen comes the first smell
Of just the gas burner being lit,
The struck match tossed into the shallow sink.

Lizards run the arbor wall.
The house settled during the war
And the faults were paved
With black pitch with clear bubbles
In it like saliva.

The delphiniums of the courtyard, the daffodils
And witchgrass are gone. Last summer
From the hill they watched the desert
And the switchbacked roads
But their father did not come home.

The bodies of seven men
Are still somewhere in the old south shaft
Of the copper mine.
They were pumping water bitter as lime.

The children listen for the mountain cats
At night. The oldest boy with a *peso*
On a string around his neck
Stares at a photograph in which

A half-frozen buffalo eats
Bunchgrass beside a hot spring, the snow
Drifting with the vapors, a geyser climbing
Into the dark winter sky. Two seasons
With a grazing margin of compromise.
He'll ask again why things die.

Lamentations

The scrub woman for the old bank and jailhouse,
Her face reddening

Over supper on a steamy night
Is thinking of the village spillway being

Answered by a dry clucking over mud, *she is
Touching the burrs on the tongue of the azalea . . .*

Exhaustion puts knotted rags in the neck
And shoulders:

As a girl, in Poland, she watched her husband
Be dragged through the shade of five pines

To the execution wall. A year earlier
She had watched him bathe

In the bronze tub the landlord had put
Out in the field as a trough for horses.

She picked him from among the men
Smoking pipes after haying, *she rolled*

*Over on her stomach
To study the blue cornflower; she shyly
Rained on the wildflowers, a hot urine . . .*
They laughed, and never knew her brother

Was taken by train to Hamburg, was infected
With tuberculosis, was

In the last days of the war
Stripped along with six other children

And hanged in the boiler room of a post office.
What she has understood

Is there are only
Two speeches the naked make well,

One is of welcome, the other farewell.

The Train

Accident could be a god to little boys.

The way they hurt their necks
To look through glass down to the twisted
Wreckage in the gorge. The conductor
Telling the ladies from Jamaica
We are one stop from the border. The older
Of the two is shocked by a sudden pasture
Beside the lake, ice houses
Left there for the summer— she says, "Oh, Chloe,
Look at the shanties; to think
There is such poverty in Maine." She begins
To finger the pearls sewn into the shoulder
Of her dress; the diamond she's wearing
Has the fire of fat in it. And then
A tunnel, and then more birches with the lake again.

You smile at me and look across
To the girl in black stockings who is asleep,
Her lips
Moving, her skirt rising with the jumping train.
You straighten your blouse. Sharing
A thermos of coffee, we have said twice
That we'll be late for the station. Beyond the window
The day-lilies are a smudged crayon.

Who is drowning in the lake? Whose father
Is falling on the stairs? Which of us
Racing north will be truly late? We are
All annoyed, stepping out into the rain.
The city that we raced for, racing for its own sake.
The girl in black stockings is waking on the corner.
She has ruined the hard parallelism of the rain.
She said her brother died in the jungle last week.
We said, with intonation, what a shame.

Old Night and Sleep

For my grandfather

A cold rain falls through empty nests, a cold rain
Falls over the canvas
Of some big beast with four stomachs
Who eats beneath a white tree
In which only a dozen dry pods are left . . .

Some new sense of days being counted.

Norman Dubie was born in Barre, Vermont, in April 1945. His poems have appeared in many magazines, including *The Paris Review, The New Yorker, The American Poetry Review, Antaeus, The Antioch Review, Field,* and *Poetry.* He has won the Bess Hokin Award of the Modern Poetry Association and fellowships from the National Endowment for the Arts and The John Simon Guggenheim Memorial Foundation. He lives in Tempe, Arizona, with his wife, Jeannine, and his daughter, Hannah. Mr. Dubie is a teacher at Arizona State University.